RAINBOW ROAD

Poems

Scott Laudati

.Bone Machine, Inc.

Earth Edition

ISBN: 8-234-06655-8
ISBN-13: 979-8-234-06655-8

BONE MACHINE, INC.
14 Allen Avenue
Manasquan, NJ 08736

ReadBoneMachine@gmail.com

Printed in the United States of America

DEDICATION

For my fellow Roman solider – Damian Rucci

Special thanks to Thom Young, Kyle Kouri, John Dorsey, Austin Manley & Matt Dabson for always keeping the foxhole warm.

“My dreams like me have all grown old
but we still dream about you,
Rainbow Road.”

- Kris Kristofferson

also by SCOTT LAUDATI

.poems.
Bone House
Camp Winapooka

.novel.
Play The Devil

RAINBOW ROAD

I.

MESEROLE & LORIMER

(Written in Brooklyn, NY)

My Bluest Valentine

Don't bake me a birthday cake
this year.
Let's go to Wawa and
buy a carton
of our old cigarettes
and drive to the Poconos,
to the mini golf
where we made dirty bets
around the windmill
and both of us got a rash
that night from the
heart-shaped hot tub.
Or we can go back
to your parents' basement
with the wood paneled walls
and the one cold night
we laid under the heater
and you whispered,
"Pretend it's Aspen."
Let's get married this time
like we swore we would at 17
when all we wanted
was to do drugs and fall in love
and we were still young enough
to be good at both.

A Garden East Of Eden

If I could do it all over again
there's not much I would do the same.
I would say I love you a lot more
to a lot less people.
I would only find brick walls on
black and white streets
to kiss against.
I would buy a shag carpet every day
and lie in it.
And I would never eat until my chest
was thin as paper
so you could see that
my heart
looks
like
a heart.

And every time I say
the house will always smell like fresh flowers
I'll mean it.
And every car door I can open for you
I'll open it.
And every cage that holds a turtle
I'll free it.
And every dog that has no home
I'll adopt it.
And every door in the house that isn't painted yellow
I'll paint it.
And every bike that has a basket
I'll fill it.
And when I promise you I'm over it
I will be.

But if I said
I don't want you to love me any more than you do
I'd still be lying,
and I'd hope that you were still smarter than me,
and you wouldn't change a thing.

Can We Live Like This?

It didn't take so long,
did it?
Your story's in your smile,
those lips once said,
"I'll never love again."

I know you're a fighter, kid.
Life didn't take it's time with you.
But you're not so bored,
there's still a light in there.
Sure,
you can sway
like the breezy palm trees
of your hometown, but
I don't want to know if you can bend ...
can you break?

I remember your greasy hair
from the plane,
your legs crossed
on the white sheets,
the slow surrender of your eyes
when you realized
I thought you were beautiful.
It was sudden and eternal.
I chose you to erase all my sorrows.
Will you?
You see life in the raw
and that makes me trust you.
We know when we find our own.

I think about what it will be like.

The coffee.
The date.
The booze.
The bed.
The cigarette.
But I can leave those for the men
that came before.
I want your window,
to watch the breeze
through the leaves of those palms
and wonder if this life actually existed
before you got here.

A Life

I used to walk around and look at alleys
or hidden corners of parks
and think,
when I've finally lost everything
I can be homeless here.

But then I got older and
left New York.
I drove through Appalachia
and the sad and stalled Midwest
and finally made it to
Montana,
where the wheat was so healthy
it was almost gold,
and no money
had ever talked to the land.
It had escaped the experiment.
It remained free.
I saw myself as a successful writer looking
out over that grass and thought,
someday when I've had enough
of this awful world
I can kill myself here.

And that's why I leave
instead of just signing the lease.
It's hard on the soul to stay.
I hit a new city like a camera
and memorize everything.
And once I've drank in all the bars
and had coffee in the morning
it's time to run.

It's the same conversation every time.
With my girlfriend,
with my mother,
that it's nothing
they did,
I just never learned
to take life
as it comes.
There's never been a past,
it's all new to me.

Maybe you know what I mean.
I've looked at women
with the old soul eyes,
who've stood on this dirt before,
and they know for sure
this is just one life
and so it will be again.
But not me.
I clocked in with clean lungs.
A boy that learned fear.
That became too sad to cry.
That didn't know
there would be a second chance.

Always remember,
if there's nothing left to lose
run for the finish line.
Always remember,
it's the fight of the century every time.
Always remember,
death
will be easier.

The Dog Days Are Over

Sometimes,
when I lose too much faith in the world -
too many wars
too many police
all going so right for the wrong,
I look at my dog
fearless
asleep
farting
shedding all over my couch.
A wild animal brought in
to serve a purpose
that went extinct
with the letter and the barn.
And I think, *"All
this animal has to do is shit
in the right place
and it makes me happy.
That's it."*
I'm pretty sure if there was a God
he would've stopped evolution
at the dog.

Of course, the dog can operate
with no regard because it
doesn't know the greatest fear -
that someday it will die.
But as animals
grow weak
and the weak are killed and eaten,
humans grow old in community homes.
And sometimes they've lost it,

and drool on bingo boards and smile
at the space between
them and time.
But usually they haven't.
And
because they are old and boring
they're stuck away
to ride out the days alone,
watching their roommates
drop out one by one.
And at the end
their very first learned lesson becomes their last -
if they want to keep everyone happy
all they have to do
is shit in the right place.

Stony Hill

The neighbors used to call the cops on us
at least
two times a week.
The other five
were the days
that we quit drinking.
I was only happy when I was with her.
We only drank
when we were together.
Sometimes
    I needed to work.
Sometimes
    she needed to paint.

I remember those days
sitting in the back of a white van,
driving from Long Island City to Wall Street,
carrying ladders and curtains
down alleys
to service elevators,
watching for the sun
to do its revolution over the
Empire State Building,
drowning itself
in the Hudson,
finally allowing
me
to drive turnpikes
and parkways
to get home
to her.

She'd wake up at five
or six.
From October to April
I don't think she ever saw
the sun.
We stole cat food so we had money for weed.
We didn't eat because of the cocaine.
    But I kept working
    and she kept sleeping.
My parents wanted to know why
she didn't get a job.
How could I explain the obvious?
She was too beautiful for work
    for orders
    for discipline
and for a girl who knows this
there's no such thing as enough.

My back hurt all the time from the grind.
My face hurt all the time from her fists.
I'll never live with a Puerto Rican again.
When she got bored she left.
When she got angry she hit.
We fought hard.
We made up hard.
    The neighbors called the law for both.
Each would leave me
bleeding
and bruised.
And when the cops showed up
it was hard to explain
    that I was actually having the best time of my life.

To The Girl I Went On A Date With Last Night

Your songs never got sadder,
how can that be?
Your mother still has your father,
you held onto your God,
I didn't know the world
still deserved something like that.

Yeah,
I'll go to Brooklyn.
I'll pay for the drinks.
I'll walk you around.
We can stand and watch the sun go down
behind
the last projects of lower Manhattan.
And I'll wonder if I invented you.
And I'll wonder if you'll erase me.
I've got the torch in my hand.
Don't turn your face too quickly,
even a breeze
will give the flames a reason to dance.

You've got the after storm blue eyes.
Your eyes tell me
you've sat on this bench before.
You know which two buildings
the sun will split.
It's the knowledge of a broken heart.
Even with your God
and your parents
love has been a betrayal.
You've spent too much time on this bench alone.

You know the bums.
You know which hipster will bring the guitar
and what song he will sing.
You can't know these things until you're alone.
And you can't be alone until you've learned
you're only safe with yourself.

It's hard to know when to make a move.
The last light has attached itself
around your head like an Icon.
The divine glow.
Whatever that yellow ring is
circling the white dove that means
peace and love
and the sun
and spring
and youth.
I know I should kiss you now
but I don't because you say,
"Let's swim to Manhattan,"
and
in the water's reflection
I realize I'd rather see you smile
than see your face touching mine.

And maybe it should end like that.
With us
not touching.
And I could know you
like the birds know the sky.
And I won't have to invent you.
And you'll never have to erase me.
Your songs will stay sweet
and we can share

the dark places of our hearts
that no one else gets to see.
I'll
love you
like only a man
who never gets the girl can,
and every day
will feel like those last minutes
we put our heads to the ground,
figuring out how to share
our first kiss
goodbye.

2:00 A.M. Or Dawn

You look over at her sleeping sometimes
and wonder
is this the last one?

Bags still packed,
clothes unwashed,
mattress still on the floor,
a leftover from the last tenant
who lived with nothing stable.
And when I lay on that mattress
my first nights in New York
I knew in my heart that love was just a relic
from centuries covered by dust,
and there was nothing left of me
to exhume those centuries
or at least find someone
who still believed.

But then you're there.
And you realize you've been there for weeks now.
And you ask yourself when it happened.
Was it the night a bartender recognized you
and put a black marker
through the bottom of the tab?
Maybe.
Or the night you choked out a taxi driver
who refused to drive her back to Manhattan?
Where have the years gone?
It was winter I think.
I remember her boot prints in the first snow.
The barista who put a shot in our coffee
for an extra dollar.

The subway kid playing "Crocodile Rock"
on a clarinet.
And how our boss didn't come to work that day
because a snow plow hit his car
so none of us did anything
and I forgot for a while
that people are inherently bad.

You look over at her sleeping sometimes
and you know you've gotten old.
You don't talk to the bartenders anymore.
You don't go anywhere with a line.
You don't feel so bad about kids in cages.
You look back and realize
you made all the wrong friends,
dated all the wrong girls,
said I love you to all the wrong people.
And it makes you exhausted
but it never makes you fall asleep.

You think about all the hearts you've been handed
and how they all came with a curse.
Except this one.
This one is still easy.
We are not the same but we are simple.
Like the "Amen" after an arduous homily,
you can bow your head and be thankful.
For the first time
asking nothing from anyone.
For the first time
happy you're here instead of anywhere else.
And if you're afraid nothing will ever be new again
just remember the last time you were free
and how you spent it all praying to be found.

II.

THE SHAPE OF POETRY TO COME

(Written on tour from Jersey to Texas)

Thus Passes The Glory Of The World

I've seen Kentucky through this windshield
three times since January.
In winter Nathan drives
and we're still tired from the night in St. Louis.
In spring I drive and I remember a story about
Whitman heading our way
before turning south.
In summer it's Tohm's turn and we stop in Wheeling
to see where the stagecoaches ran out of road,
before the bridge was built,
and now it has collapsed.
The grass is never blue but the river's always brown.
I haven't read a book written by a stranger
in over a year.
Every time I get into a car there's a destination.
It's not like walking.
I always know where I'm going.
On Sunday we rob a grocery store and get out
with three burritos and a six pack.
Tohm is taking us fast through the Allegheny Tunnel
and I use my lighter to open two beers.
Will we sleep better tonight?
Who lives inside these highway trailers?
There are red lights appearing before us like deer eyes
wide and lost under a setting sun.
I don't say slow down.
We can sleep forever rubbed on this asphalt.
We can dream in sentences buried beneath it.

The Ohio Line

This is a country of rivers fed by sewer mains,
and our grievances roll with them
from the high bluff on one side
down to the new valley ahead.
We never cross back the other way in daylight.
The houses in the hills always at our backs.
I can see all the past lives in the rearview:
frontier men inventing American poverty,
Shawnee being dragged west
to an everlasting purgatory,
women cooking worms by the recipes
of their mothers.
The generations who dug their hands
into the soil of this final second chance,
losers lapping up a promise
that has since rolled back.
There are no children left to fall off the cliff.
All dirt roads are etched
to the direction of a single highway.
And now these towns have submitted back to jungle.
My home has never collapsed
and so I have nowhere
to leave my fears.
Next time we'll start the tour out west
and the sins of all my unkempt graves
will dig deeper lines on this drying face.
I know now there's no escape
from a strong Ohio wind
looking for a fresh wound to burrow deep.

Scenic Columbus

In Columbus I eat mushrooms and
ask to see something beautiful.

Ezhno takes me to the overpass above
the highway and says,

"This is the perfect place to throw
Molotov cocktails down at cops."

Portsmouth, Ohio

There's no place for wildlife
if animals like these roam the cities.
The country is on the precipice of its next riot
and the Casey's is fresh out of cheese pizza.
I used to think about places like Tunisia
and Medellin when I thought this life was fair
and these words would take me outside
of ghettos and the last stop on the A Train.

But those dreams leave your head first.
There's a quick first love and then the rest of you life.
How many dollar slices can one stomach take?
Are these fair thoughts
when you're sitting in a theater
the punks of Portsmouth managed to reclaim?
I'm a lucky man.
I wrote a book and then I got to see the country.

I brush my teeth on a deserted street and
think about my father's face when I told him
I'd quit my union job and was driving 400 miles
to read poems for six minutes in Ohio.
A shopping cart bum passes behind me in silence.
His throat unslit, his eyes greyed by time.
What's the point of locking the car?
There's nothing of our lives anyone
would want to steal.

The tears of an empire have dried up.
We don't cry.
We're not curious.
Is there a girl in Tunisia who dreams of Los Angeles?

American's don't even see America.
But the sun still hangs over Portsmouth,
the babies smile here like they do in every womb,
and the single string of a violin sounds sad
whether you're on the rooftops or in the street,
the last one to call a city home
or the first one on the bus out.

Behind The Belle Motel

I'm 35 taking a piss outside a
purple house in Belle, Missouri.
This is our off day. I'm supposed to be asleep.
Recovering.
But I could hear the couple behind the
Belle Motel all morning.
I thought of myself as a person who would
get involved in a mess like this.
Who'd save people. Who'd do the right thing.
But I'm not. I'm a person who says,
"If he takes one more step, I'll do something."
Then he does and I say, "All right,
if he lifts his hands I'll do something."
Then he does and she's lying in the dirt
holding her jaw while three little blonde kids
cry and scream for their mother.
I'm a person who says, "Now someone else will
definitely show up and stop this."
But no one does. She gets up, tells her crying kids
to shut the fuck up, and they all go inside. To recover.
An American family who can't afford to get divorced.
A success story in the margins of statistics.
It's nine a.m. and I'm 35 and hungover.
I pour my coffee on the bush I just watered
to kill the smell.
Then I go inside and fall into bed.
Look under the pillows for bugs.
Punch my restless legs.
Know from the start it is hopeless.
I'm never recovering. I'm always reducing.
Faster as time bleeds on.

Farmhouse On The Gasconade

It's a warm January in these Ozark foothills.
There is no land like this back east,
there are no people like this either.
If you feel hunted do not come here,
this is where the hunters write their poetry.

This deck I'm standing on overlooks
a brown and fast moving river.
Two brown and fast moving dogs
emerge from it, a bone with fur
and dripping veiny blood is held between
both of their jaws, and they roll and tug
and wag their tails like they've just
caught the last deer in Missouri.

It wasn't a crime 200 years ago to rid these hills
of the Osage, but there's blood out here that digs
deeper than the roots of these skinny Oaks.
It's stronger than the currents of these brown rivers.
It comes at night when you drive back to town.
The road you left on doesn't drop you off
where you found it. Doors swing open
untouched by the wind. Everyone knows the
same secret though they'd never share it.

The hunters will expire in one or two more floods
and all the old men will be gone,
forgotten and unpraised.
But the Sasquatch at the bottom of the hill
has raised his family here for generations.
He has outlasted the Osage, and he will outlast us.
Scorched treaties. Indignant hands. Last words.

He awaits the liturgy of the kingfisher,
a cannon shot to signal the
nothingness of a nothing world
finally being reinherited by its rightful servants.

Tonight, It's Indiana!

The stage was warm tonight and finally
someone had heard of me before I faced the crowd.
There's a love story I never tell but I gave it away
in Indianapolis and every heart in that room
remembered its first surrender.
Too bad you can't bank whatever magic appears
in the sacred basements of Midwest commissaries.
The wet sponge rests on your head
and the immortality of tonight never means
tomorrow will be better.
There is no life for 2nd place.
You leave the stage and the Old Style's
replace high fives.
You don't have to crash with the gutter punks
because when you do well the bartender
remembers he has an air mattress in his living room.
The girl who hated New York before
you got on the mic
now wants to know all about the city.
And you can give yourself two hours
to revel in the good life
because you found the only way
to live in the moment.
And tomorrow when you wake up in
the cold room of an old Victorian
the sun will cut through the blinds like gold bars.
And the cat who shares your pillow
will remind you of a warm bed you slept in once
where the dreams came easy
and everything that hurt could still be forgiven.

Just 300 Miles To Salina

Those men under the piers they spit silica
but it never comes out as easy as it went in.
The dust hides little anchors
and even after the job is done they hang around
like Christmas ornaments still up in July.
Some things decay much faster than others.
Nothing is uglier than the trail to Salina.
I tried to skip the middle chapters
but the compass only pointed one direction.
Were those years on the docks worth the cold?
The ice water getting between my gloves and sleeves.
Eating pills to stave off the pain.
Praying for a low tide so I wouldn't drown
if I fell off the barge.
And now my father won't talk to me.
The beginning and end mean nothing to him,
the pain of the middle is the glory.
Damian punches my arm and I ask
how far we are from Salina.
Just 300 miles.
I've seen the country now
and I've forgotten most of it,
but not that landscape between us and Salina.
The American Sahara.
The space where all things found the middle
and civilization rolled back.
A place no one has ever missed.
I can think so clearly when there's no one listening.
I even remember how unawed the antelope looked
kneeling under the mothership's beam.
Once upon a time all land looked like this land
and it won't be long now before it all does again.

We Write Poems About Bullshit

They write poems about polyamory in Kansas City.
They write poems about guys
who couldn't make them cum in Lawrence.
They write poems about gun fights in Little Rock.
They write factory poems everywhere.
I write love poems about a Puerto Rican girl
who stabbed me 15 years ago.
I write poems about aliens and my dog
and absolutely nothing important,
but I never write about girls with hoop earrings
and Staten Island accents
in Ugg Boots and sweatpants
with "Juicy" stitched across the ass
even though it's what I've spent almost
my entire life thinking about.

We all write nothing but bullshit
and no one who isn't trying to be a poet themselves
will ever read any of this nonsense anyway.

What Does Your Couch Smell Like?

I only think about sleep now.
Not the afterparty
or the stage
or what part of my poem
I should yell at the audience
to trick them into thinking
what I'm saying is important.
I had a love seat in Kansas City
that sagged in the middle.
The bed three people had hung themselves
above in Belle.
The air mattress in St. Louis was okay but after
a bottle of Jameson and 10 Budweiser's
so is anywhere.
When I was young this was all I wanted,
to see every statue in every square,
Confederate or conqueror, it didn't matter.
All I know now is the parking lots,
how to dry a towel on a backseat,
which barista is most likely to give me a free beer.
It's all material for the great story, right?
All I have to do is write it.
A day off in Oklahoma, maybe.
A white pillow under my head then
coffee from anywhere but a gas station.
When did I get too old for any of this to matter?
I have to collect 1000 nights to write a poem,
and none of them end in a good night's sleep.

From The Backseat Of Stolte's Car

I love the Midwest because things that
come and go back east stay here,
probably longer than they should,
but long enough to hold and make some sense of.

The tents under the overpasses aren't just canvas
that disappear and pop back up on a different road.
You see them day after day and
learn the sleep schedules,
how the dog tied up deals with the cold,
who's moved in since yesterday.

The pizza place with the thumb tack
menu board above the counter
has prices from when it opened next to today's.
You can almost touch what's been stolen from you.
But the pinball machine is still $0.25.
Life makes sense, and you know what?
It's not all bad.

I feel like I only meet people I hoped I'd never meet.
Why have I seen so many cities
no one from New York has ever seen?
I thought I was the chosen one for so long,
the Uncle Sam of my time,
a duty to walk from town to town
like Johnny Appleseed and tell them
where I'd come from
then go home and explain what I'd seen.

I've been looking for the real America
since I learned to read,

staring at trains and busses knowing they were going
to places a little closer to the beating heart.
But now I'm standing on the banks of the muddy
and shallow Miami River and I can't pretend
I haven't found the Rosetta Stone over and over:
the secret truth is just money.
It's not art or family or a basset hound
that wants it's ears scratched.
It's just money.
And if you weren't born with it
you're never going to have it.
And if you don't have it
you're never going to sit at the table.

I love the Midwest because it's always known this.
It doesn't even try to fight for the scraps.
It's an honorable place for a man to
find some shade and lie down.
Everyone knows it's been a shell game since
the first Indian signed the first treaty.
It's why no one's first instinct is to call the police.
It's why they hand you a gun
before you drink your first beer.
It's better for all of us to get the game over
so we can finally go home.

Driving To Thom Young's House

I heard there were no gun laws in Texas
so I rented a Taurus and drove
to Thom Young's house,
running over prairie dogs and singing the new
Blake Shelton Christmas song.
And when I got there
I bought a rifle and some nightcrawlers
and we fished in a puddle behind the Allsup's.
But the fish didn't want any worms
and on the drive back
Thom said Led Zeppelin wouldn't make it today.
And I remembered the music
and how it had lived in me once
and in my dreams
I can still hear my mother sing it like
she's hanging over my crib.
And sometimes the college radio
comes in clear from Amarillo
and Thom finds an old box of tobacco
and we smoke like Kings without a throne,
flicking ash at the coyotes circling the porch,
once upon a time betting on
whether it would be them
or us
but we don't play that game as much anymore.
And on cold Sundays after Christmas
we leave burritos outside for the dogs.

Clayton, NM

I saw the VFW in downtown Clayton
and watched the past lay naked
around an unplugged jukebox
while the first drop of rain in six years
hit the window
just before happy hour.

Sad spit
from the big blue monster.
Always above.
Holding nothing of God.
Never smiling at the peasants below
still kneeling on roads
they'd run cattle down
when dew grew the crop
and the rivers
rushed with gold.

Luckily, I found a $0.50 postcard
at Goodwill
so I could write home
and tell my mom
that I'd seen the end now -
the scalped heads impaled
on the picket fences,
the weatherproof eviction tags,
and the bagpipes they hadn't even blown
because there was no one left
to hear them.

The Greyhounds all drove on
to Trinidad

and the prairie dogs
looked to the buzzards
and begged them,
"Please,
just make it quick."

The December Of Lost Poets

There isn't a gas station bathroom
a poet hasn't pissed in
There isn't a field that hasn't been puked in
There isn't a rust belt
where dinner hasn't been skipped
No highway a poem wasn't written
No river a cigarette didn't swim
No couch that wasn't slept on
No diner a eulogy wasn't spit

They invented the car
The highway
The gas station
The Slurpee
The french fry
The napkin
and they invented the poets who write on them.

But they didn't make a guardian angel of lost scrolls.
No creature crawled out of the campfire to chase
taillights down highways like dogs and boys
screaming for a way out.
The words and their men drag from backseats
and parade through Main Street like conquistadors
always from a far away home,
leaving art and desecrated facades and hopefully
a few converts to see again on their next voyage west.
And then they get back in the car,
the words remembered or forgotten,
the poets homeless or employed, but nothing
to collect the blood and pages from notebooks
that meet their ends on the highway nights

from Pittsburgh to Louisville.

And then they're home,
trying to sum it all up in a conversation,
remembering it's always hot but somehow
it's also always December,
wondering why they pulled the jukeboxes out
at every truck stop
and who's eating all the apple pie in Iowa?
And asking how could everyone be Irish
but no one is singing these pirate tales
over pints of frothing ale,
giving a lifetime of sacrifice some meaning
or at least a spot in the history books or ghost stories
so on the right night they can come alive again
and convince the kids the road
is more than an executioner -
it is a fountain of youth that kills you smiling.

You'll die early because once you've found it
there's nothing left to search for.
It's the third rail of the Universe
and a good shot of it will push you
through the portal.
Haven't you ever wondered why poets
never die in their sleep?
Your curse is to limp from town to town
until the fabric can be stitched back together.
Maybe in Clovis. Maybe in Cherokee.
Never refuse a needle and thread.
Don't forget, you can't be killed if you don't lie down,
but the American grass makes a nice pillow
if you need to rest your head for just a minute.

III.

DROP THE BOMB ALREADY

(Written in Suncroft, Ireland)

Grit

They all want to be artists.
They change their majors
from psychology to sculpting.
They change later
from sculpting to economics.
Their parents say, "Get a job. Save money.
You can work your art out on the weekends."
Most give in.
Get the job.
They sleep around in their twenties.
They get pregnant.
Sometimes for love.
Usually by accident.
They get promoted.
They become their refrigerator.

Some stay on.
Move to the Dominican neighborhoods.
Move to the outer boroughs.
Keep hustling.
Always one contact away from the big gallery.
Thinking they made the sacrifice.
  Art owes them now.
  One day it will happen.

But it doesn't,
or when it does it's just too late.
Too much time happened to question,
playing the ultimate gamble
with no chance to return
and get it right
or rewind and try again.

But they bet their lives
and the ashtrays never emptied
and the bottles never corked
and they left something behind,
good or bad
they wrote their own epitaphs.
And the graveyards
and libraries
and art galleries
all filled
because the artist lived
and the artist left something behind.
But whether the dream was lived out
or sold out
it's hard to see a family
on a blanket under a free sky
every July 4th,
or around a Christmas tree every December,
or taking a picture
with Mickey Mouse in the Florida summer,
and argue
that the love you gave your name
isn't the only art
worth waking up for.

What Were You Good At?

I don't remember when it started
but the end came last Tuesday.
I'd taken a Xanax and slept all day,
seeing an old girlfriend
and my dead dog
in dreams or nightmares
or some other Hell that I'll get to relive
if I don't get this life right.
And when I finally woke
I couldn't ignore what all the bad poems
and awful music had been telling me:
I'd lived too long,
there aren't going to be new chapters in my book,
there won't be any more songs.
This can happen to some at ninety
and others at thirty.
But I think for most it never happens
and that's why rational people still breed
without any fear
of consequence.
Don't they see the holes in everything?
Don't they know there's no Second Coming?
Most people start dying from the minute
they're born. It
took me thirty-five years to give up
and sometimes
I'm still proud of that.
The world didn't want a new poet,
but there's always room for another plumber.

Songs For The New War

I've heard songs for the new war.
They chant over crank radios
like heartbeats from a shaman's drum.
They come out of subways on
a three-string guitar
and the words of a runaway
who still believes in his favorite band.
They live in hog squeals you can hear from
rooftops in Chicago,
trapped in perdition,
riding the currents of the universe
like a crest without a trough.

These are the songs for the new war.
I heard my first from a Rat King
who ended his sermon with,
"Humans have infinite past lives ...
but animals get none."
I heard my second in a dream where
a black moon rose over a shallow lake
and tadpoles swam circles around the reflection
like black stars in orbit.
Is this what gets lost when we die?
Does the melody cling too tight to your soul?
What if you kept in no tears
and never found a lie you didn't tell?
Anyone who ever lived,
any martian who ever visited,
any elephant who ever buried its friend,
it's all led to this.
And when the messenger arrives
no one will ask about

his chest full of arrows.
And no one will care about the conclusion
of free will.

The songs of the new war will fade out
before their last chords.
They won't be hummed in the FEMA camps
or by the future Reichs.
They'll be buried like the family dog,
mourned for an hour
then immediately replaced.

What Was Your Sin?

What was your sin?
Were you born poor on this end of America?
Did you notice a new vein
while the traffic camera flashed and
your knuckles scraped against the asphalt?
Palms always up so
the Voodoo Lady on the corner
could get a read.
She ran The Grange once
but they lock her up now for
practicing without a permit.
A bum by the bodega saw
the arrest and said,
"They would've charged Jesus Christ
for a fishing license if it got
a dollar out of him."

She didn't care about their rules, though.
She saw her God in the exhaust
behind the city bus.

We watched from the fire escape
and Haitian women
brought her sticks and frogs
they'd stolen from the pet store.
The Voodoo Lady boiled it all in a bucket
outside the Crown Fried Chicken
and when it turned green
everyone stuck a straw in
and took a nice big gulp.
They had black incense smoking
and a cat

they were about to skin
when the cops taped off the street.
A fat one put his boot on the bucket
and tipped the potion over
and as the green slime swam
for the sidewalk cracks
every fly in New York
showed up for dinner.
The cops handcuffed the Voodoo Lady
and she said to them,
"I'm the last Saint of Harlem.
That used to mean something."

We tried to go back but never tried to grow up.
Remember, your great-grandfather wasn't
Thomas Jefferson -
even with all those student loans
you'll never be one of them.
And don't tell anyone you have the
slave blood running through you;
give them your heart
and they'll still bury you
on the other side of the fence.

It's everything a fairy tale isn't.
Those ivory keys were carved
from whales' teeth.
These were the lessons of our youth
but your fingers never mainlined
the right vibe.
You think your luck is all bad
but remember,
you can still watch the sunset,
and that car you bought held up pretty good

after you killed your boss
over a weekend shift.
Did you look back at the cart-boy?
He doesn't mean it
but he can't help making a "peace sign"
at the worst times.

The real hero rides shotgun and
smiles at the geckos,
while the good people wash dishes
and load their rifles.
And remember,
when the call comes
the Voodoo Lady said
they'd try and write down your license plate.
So drive fast, it won't be long before
they go blind
from the sunset.
And eventually you'll look like a comet,
and they'll wonder
if you came out the other side.

The Final Act

Look outside,
there's a little sun left over the bay.
If you're still hungry stick a hook through my lip
and cast me out.
I'll hold my breath and sink to the bottom,
dig my feet into the sand
until a clam bites my big toe.
If I find enough we can take the catch
to New York
and sell it on the old Bowery.
There's a tent there with a tank
full of dead manatees called
The Mermaid Mausoleum.
My mom took me to see it on my sixth birthday.
The ticket came with a free photograph
and a piece of Bubble Yum.
Maybe my picture is still on the wall.
Maybe we can refill my well of hate
that's been running dry for years.
The sun's gone down now.
No planes.
No moon.
It's seemed like the end of my whole life, I think.
And tonight I'll go to sleep under stars
dead before the first man,
wondering why it's taken so long for us,
hoping the credits roll soon.

Fish Tank

I believed in everything
when I was twenty
except when you told me
your tree had been cursed.
The Dow Jones crashed that day
or maybe
it was before the end of all things,
back when we watched Saddam's body double
drop through the floor
and the crowd cheered
as the noose tightened.
We didn't look away from the computer screen
and I don't think I did again
until your mom showed up and
dumped my fish tank
full of fancy guppies down the toilet.
You packed your YSL heels back in the box
while I yelled at your mom
and no one listened
as I explained how hard it had been
to get those fish to breed.
No one listened at the bar that night either.
And I guess you were right,
love's only a cure until it becomes a regret.
But you could've just left a note when you
decided to break my heart.
I don't know why the fish had to die, too.

The Leader

I've seen an unspilt tongue sting like an arrow
across a fold-up table where drink rings
formed galaxies
and myths rose and fell
until the singer of songs collected his favorites,
wrung them out like a wet towel,
watched the words spill onto the pavement
like rain drops,
and there they swam until he picked up his favorites
and pinned them onto the pages
of trailer park scripture.

Were there days like these in Roman times?
Did the hare ever outrun the hounds?
There's genius in his war, but there's hate in the trees,
they don't tremble in the wind anymore.
The waterbed sprung a leak.
The government lost the bread order.
The knife truck only sharpens scissors.
There's a place called Malibu
but no one here has ever seen it.
It might as well be a retirement plan or Arcadia.
They know the chopping block, though.
They know what it's like to beg for a clean kill.

Always at The Arbiter's table
sit the naked and the frugal.
Infants submerge quietly in his tub.
Pilgrims sleep soundly under his tree.
His knife need not be sharpened,
a snow-drift of mayonnaise spreads along the host
and open mouthed they line up one by one.

A gas bill unpaid, but warmth from somewhere.
A family tree burned, but a King still emerged.
The featherbed awaits.
The indentation of a pretty young thing still asleep.
Enjoy it now. You'll have to die for it.
But you've always known this,
I think.

Putting The Art Back In Kmart

When we were young
rocks were the thing to throw.
It taught me a lot about glass
(sand and soda).
Sometimes the rocks
would sail through nice and clean,
and only a small hole
the size of a golf ball or
baseball was made, like bullets
spraying across a plaster wall.
Other times the glass would shatter
off in huge chunks
(like countries falling from a map)
and hit the floor.
It made the sound of a wave crashing
on a dirty beach.
  I guess the more chemicals,
  the shittier the glass.

Car windows were my favorite,
especially
the windshields.
We dropped boulders from trees.
We put rocks
into potato guns.
We even ran and cannonballed.
But the windshields never broke open,
and nothing
ever got through.
Instead
these beautiful designs formed –
rings over water,

a thawing pond,
a map of the galaxy.
And after we were sweaty and bleeding
we'd look at our abstraction.
A used car lot turned into a modern art gallery.
    Sometimes we took pictures.

In high school they made us take art class.
We learned a lot about the old masters,
and they were good,
but there always seemed
to be some element missing.
The mad flash.
The knife or the canvas.
It never got through.

THE ASSIGNMENT
was to be creative:
"You can do anything that inspires you."
So we got canvas,
threw paint at it,
pissed on it,
dropped our burning cigarettes,
someone even jerked off on it.
But it was still lame
and nothing
to be proud of.

We took mushrooms to get deeper,
and like mushrooms usually do,
we went out into the woods.
I only remember the spider webs,
big webs,
lactating silk

like pure fresh squeezed milk.
They were so lush I wanted to eat them.
  So I did.

I woke up in a hospital two days later
with a fever,
delirious,
and covered in huge red bites.
No real memory of what happened
but they told me
I had said, "The spiderwebs look
just like broken glass."
My friends were inspired.
After they called an ambulance
they went to smash a car windshield
and bring it in for our
"Inspiration Project."
But we weren't
nine anymore -
too much Taco Bell
and cigarettes
will cut "fleeing the scene"
to "complying
with the law"
very quickly.
  Everyone
  who didn't go to the hospital that night
  went to jail.

Our teacher was fired the next Monday.
Her replacement had a psych degree
and we spent the rest of the year
gluing pasta together.
  We were all safe after that

but none of us went on
to make something
anybody would ever stop and look at.

No Future

They laugh at me at weddings
at reunions
at the 7-11 and probably
in the backyards where we used words like
best friends and *someday*.
I'm their jester now.
The one who puts it on the line
for their amusement.
Like drinking in these caves is easy.
Like I wanted to carve words onto paper
that didn't resonate with anyone.

It's open season on the weak.
The waitress
the deli girl
the ones who write poems in their own blood
and give them out for free.
Should the naked be hunted
just because they walked outside?
Don't look for sympathy in the smiles,
it's been a gamble
since the first "Amen."

I know this was all for nothing now.
I should've listened to my father
back when there was still
an exit off this road.
Back when I wanted to live much longer
than I do now.
Back when I felt the fire
and lived like it was never going
to burn out.

We Need The Bomb

We turned on the TV
and they said
we have the bomb,
they have the bomb,
the ones to the north and the west
have the bomb,
but now THEY
are trying to get the bomb,
and when they do
the world will finally
go out as it came in –
the cataclysm of
fission and fusion
and all the fury
of a billion years of anger
(the madness of good men),
and with their deaths
will go the anger
as it gets brought
back to the place –
wherever that place is
that anger comes from.

I was stoned enough
to be afraid
but you sat with me
and drank something made
for a vacation we never went on
and you said, "Well,
we better get the bomb before they do,"
as you took me
to the bedroom,

and for the first time
you were violent
and you were terrifying
and the wall shook
as I went blind
with helpless orgasm.

I'm not sure what the bomb
will look like
on the day all the leaders get together
and decide to play a big game
of dodgeball.
But for the Andromedans
on the mothership
and the reptilians
watching
from the moon –
it'll probably look like the earth
going blind
with helpless orgasm.

The Basement Days

His parents
let us smoke
in their basement
and we played music
and drank all night
and pretended
we were asleep
while his dad
got ready for work.
And once he left
we'd start painting again
until the very last
dark corner
of the window
was taken by the sun
and then we'd collapse
in exhaustion.

Time always against us.

I can't remember
what the rush was then
or where the drive
came from
but we
never looked
at those four walls
and the
warm heater
and the tea
his mother made us
with anything but

fear.

Fear
of those parties in Brooklyn
we weren't at.
Fear of a whole life
in front of us
and missing
a single cobblestone street in
a world that wasn't
too big yet.
A fear I can only
see on my dog's face
when I say, "I'll
be right back."
The unknown.
The missing.
The *what will we become?*

We left
that basement
as fast as we could.
Left the suburbs
for landlords
who won't let us
smoke inside.
And now
it's just bars.
To face your life
in the mirror
of a bar bathroom
again
and again,
it's just too big.

We had a basement
and tea once.
We were tremendous
and the world
outside the door
was small.

Smoking and painting,
just waiting for a sunny June
to finally live all the plans
we'd made in winter.

We were giants once
and the world
was small.

Give A Lozenges To The Voice Of The Archangel

They called me at work and told me
about a rainy New Jersey morning
about a bed full of vomit
about a dead kid
and a mailbox just out front
stuffed with cards
saying,
"Happy 20th Birthday."

Some people
wanted to know why.
They asked God.
They asked the quiet boys in the back
what they knew.
But what could they say?
There's only one way
a kid dies
when there's no car crash.

We heard it was a Persian connection
whose cousin or father ran the oxy ring.
So they jumped in the car
so mad
and red eyed
their heads would have to be
removed from their bodies
to stop the hate from swinging.
But when they found the Persian dealer
he didn't fight back.
He just cried.
And that was all it took for the hate to stop.

They saw something so black,
the thing that exists
in the corner of all eyes,
the thing we all sleep with,
and when we recognize it in others
it becomes impossible
to pretend your tribe
is not
my tribe.
So there they were,
putting the safety back on,
letting humanity get in the way
of revenge again.

We called him "Little"
(He shared his father's name)
and before the oxy's
and the New Jersey highway nights
he planted a seed
in his parents' backyard
that sprouted up a little maple tree.
I don't know why
I always think of that.
When people grow up
you only remember them for
the times
they've fucked you over
or fucked her before you did.
But when you get them young
it's
the times they reminded you
there's still some beauty left in the world
that stay with you.

The funeral proved a betrayal
worthy of a new scripture.
Three blonde angels
cried at the casket
and screamed what we all know
but never say -
  there is no God.
They buried him in a t-shirt and jeans
because he was a kid
and he was cool
and honoring him
in an honest way
kept everyone honest,
nobody could lie and say
he'd gone to a better place.
I cried for the first time as a man
and it felt like one more tattoo
had been hammered
onto
the surface of my heart.

Back at my aunt's
she held me for too long.
She said,
"I lost my little boy.
He always looked up to you."
All I could say was,
"He was a cool kid."
And I looked at my aunt
who had lost her little boy.
And my uncle,
a bulldog of a man
life had finally beaten.
And my three blonde cousins

who might've been thinking
about the day he was born,
or the men
they would marry
that would never share the altar
with their brother.
And I thought
about all the friends
I've had
that died or went to jail
and the reason
was always the same: heroin.
And once again
I hadn't seen the signs
that were now
so obvious,
and I never reached out
even though
everyone needs it.
When I looked outside
I could see the seed
"Little" had planted
was now a full grown tree,
but nobody mentioned it.

I went home
and
my girlfriend said,
"Throw them out.
Take a break.
Hasn't enough happened?"
I told her I did
but I didn't.
I ate them.

All of them.
And I drank.
I knew I might die
but
I probably wouldn't,
and at least
I would feel better for a while.
I should've told "Little"
about what the suburbs and
boredom will do.
But he was a smart kid,
we shared the same blood.
I should've told him
about the edge
and what going over it will do
to everyone you leave behind.

IV.

NONE BUT THE SACRED

(Written in Jamestown, RI)

My Suitcase Is Packed

I know you're home somewhere out there
in Colorado
where the desert flowers
wait all year to turn yellow
and horses with Spanish blood
whip their manes under lightning
as the snows melt down to refill
dried beds.
Somewhere where enough was enough
and you had to put a continent between me
and New Jersey.
I've seen that land and pulled over
to swim naked
where the white crests shatter
and freedom is something more
than a dream.
There are no dead ends on your streets,
the rain only falls straight down
and even stray cats
come when they're called.
I bled for you once
when the war was still far from over
and the end hasn't gotten any closer
so I guess
I'd do it again.

Cypripedium Reginae or Lady Of The Holler

I saw God once in the fingertips of a woman.
She understood the white keys
on a 1975 Fender Rhodes
the way a poet knows a typewriter
when the heart's found the right words.

It was in a cabin on the border
between
West Virginia and Maryland.
Between who we were
and what we would be.

Between nothing and nowhere.

It hadn't rained all year
and they said it was likely to stay that way,
but we didn't have any hope to begin with
so bad news came
like a report card
from a class we'd already quit.
And I'm pretty sure we both
would've already killed ourselves
if we didn't care so much
about the ones we'd leave behind.

A thunderstorm hit the house that night
but it didn't bring any rain.
And we finished a bottle
of Kentucky Gentleman
while the lights flickered
and cast shadows around the room.

My hands tried to stay focused
and slide between
the A# and F chords
as we sang the chorus of
"Peace In The Valley" slow,
less like a spiritual
and more like Johnny and June.

The walls shook in that old house
and every tree out in the holler
echoed back in evil choir.
The hard bark ground together
like a bow on rusty strings,
no leaves on their branches
(like dead fingers reaching for the clouds).

She came like a deity into that basement
and I believe she was fighting off something
deep in the bush
because
she sang at the microphone
like the words were a weapon
that she had birthed and held close.
It was one of those moments
that inspires scripture -
a burning bush
a parting sea
(I saw *IT* in her voice)
and even though we never touched
we made a kind of love
that crosses oceans like
letters and birds
like
dolphins and boats.

Our producer needed to check the mix
so we went outside
and she counted lightning bolts and centuries
in the lines of my palms.
The sidewalk was covered in broken glass
reflecting under the streetlights
like jewels never mined from the pavement.
I kicked some of it out of the way
to give her a path to walk
but she was one of those Appalachian Queens
grown up from hard dirt,
she let me be a gentleman
but she didn't need my help.
She came out that night in
Doc Martens
and a Sunday dress.
Born with a Marlboro Red in her mouth
and raised on
government cheese,
her kind was immune to things
like crushes and the cold.

"Do you think all our good years are gone?" I asked.
"Oh yeah," she said. "I've got a kid now and
I'm finally in control."
She smiled while she said it
and in a ditch between
the road and a corn field
a little purple flower
swayed lonely and afraid.
It was a lady's-slipper orchid
(The rarest flower in West Virginia).

"Look," I pointed at the flower,

"that's more scarce than gold."
And we laughed as she held
her foot against it and said,
"If I had slippers like this
I'd never need new shoes."
I looked at her for a long time
like I had something to say,
and she must've read my mind
because she said, "No, you don't,"
and I didn't argue,
I just agreed.

It rained the next morning
and when the sun came back
we walked to the lady's-slipper.
It's green stalk was bare
and a few purple petals
were pressed into the asphalt
like old pieces of gum.
I looked at her again and
she said, "You think love is ever permanent?
You can't even count on the drought
to stay loyal."

God didn't give her wings
but He taught her how to sing.
And maybe love isn't forever,
but a song is.
And on nights like this -
when the winter
hymns blow loud through the trees -
I play that old song on my guitar
and think about her,
grown up from that West Virginia holler.

And that flower,
grown up from the same West Virginia dirt.

She was an angel for sure.
I don't know why I didn't see it before.

The Woolly Mammoth

Remember back when you were young?
You thought you'd get a diploma
the old-fashioned way.
The first voice of a new generation
screaming "Get me out of here"
or "I want to go home."
I heard it down hallways
before we rolled dice
on the bathroom floor.
I heard it like a slave hears
new religion raining from the trees.
From homeroom to the Principal's office,
they tried to take it out, arrest your rage,
but it stunk up every vein in your body
like a clogged sewer,
and you were never afraid to lose it.
"In the womb," you told me once,
"I was unhappy even then."

And then there were the streets.
The bus station in Newark
and the park two blocks down
where the runaways raid
the pigeon coops and
they find dead bums
and cigarette butts dragged out.
It was like a vacation home right on a river,
under buildings like dead peaks so the sun
never shined into your eyes.

It was so you,
every move planned for the great story.

Those were the days you were always
looking forward to.
The envy of every fool.
You wrote your own legend
and it kept me amused.
I used to think that was pretty cool
but I'm invisible now,
I'll fade away
like the woolly mammoth
but you …
you'll live on forever as
some kind of Cinderella,
or the pin-up girl.

The Heart Of America

I lost another one who didn't want love
or forever
or some way back to
the heart of America.
She just wanted kids.
White kids
named John and Jesse and little Sally.
Kids that would get her off work
and never make her think
about California
and giraffes
or the way she felt at 16
when her parents stopped loving her
but said the words anyway,
who looked at their little girl
and decided she didn't have *it*
so they went to the next one.

She wanted kids who'd adopt a dog
named Lady or Molly,
and a vet who might say, "It's a 1/4 pit bull
but the dog will never stop looking like a Lab."
And the house could be new.
And the kids would never have
their own minds.
They would be patriots
and they would never fail like citizens.
Their mother could change the truth
and never have to explain
that she'd found love once
and it didn't act
like it was supposed to,

that she didn't say, "Hit me"
while age and time were still on her side.

The kids would never want to know
about the heart of America
and how it disappeared
just around the time
they made it cool
to sell love
for money.

Mick And Keith

I hated gallery openings.
There were usually a few girls,
sure,
but they were
"artists waiting for inspiration."
So,
while waiting for whatever
Divine Intervention comes
to paint people's canvases for them,
the girls brought the cocaine
and they lay on their
backs pretty easy.

She came up to me at my first show
and said,
"I know you're going to break my heart."
She hadn't cut her bangs yet
(though she would),
and she hadn't shed her winter fat
(though she would),
but I kissed her anyway
because I'm easy
and I understand why women
leave bars with men
who look like they were born old
and had never been boys
in love.
It's the same reason I kissed her -
she gave me something.
I just needed to feel like
I mattered that night
and I knew I mattered to her.

There was a joke she didn't have to tell
to make me laugh.
With her it felt like high school -
they were all against us
and we were winning.
She'd make me write.
Her desk was filled with
ashtrays
and the whitest lines
and French books from the 60's
written by names I pretended to know.
I'd type a paragraph
and show her
and she would shriek
and the dog would jump on
it's back legs
and they would dance around me
like shamans
whose chants had actually brought rain.

It was never morning.
She could spin the moon
so the night lasted forever.
An entire winter
of good cocaine,
an
immortal beauty,
and a black dog.
I never had any money
but she didn't care.
She kept cooking,
kept supplying,
and I kept promising
that someday when I made it

all the dedications would be hers.

The artists all loved her.
No one had any money
and we all needed
booze
and drugs
and love
and she gave it
(never
asked for anything in return).
The spoils were mainly mine
and I'd promise her things
but I never stopped taking.
And one night she cried
and
begged me to never leave her.
And of course
I said okay.

But we never robbed the bank together.
And we didn't steal that car
and drive to California.
She needed
a life
that was hers.
It was the first time I saw
fear in her eyes.
Our scene couldn't operate without her
but the world could live
without our scene.
I'd tell her someday
the readers would know what she did.
At our worst she held us

like the mother
most of us were missing.
And then one day I left
and
I didn't think much of what
her life would be without me
because
I never thought much of myself.

Now it's all I think about -
what a promise means.
She made the world a better place,
maybe two people in history
could say that.
And then there was the last night
when I finally found my voice
and I said, "Fuck this whole world,"
and left.

There's still a lot of night.
Still dogs.
Still blow.
But
Air and Water signs
they've never been so separate.
It doesn't feel like high school now.
They're still against us
but that's
no victory anymore.

I watched her dance the Fado
and drink the sad wine.
But people can't just let go
and that was something

we were worse at.
We fixed our hearts
but they broke
just as easy -
left in poems and pictures
for our children to think
we lived happy lives.

I still drink the sad wine
and if I try
I don't think of her sometimes.

My Friend Tom

My friend Tom always understood me,
even at the times
when I scared
myself.
I was always screaming for an audience
up on a guitar amp
and then I'd drink too much
and quiet down from the pills.
Tom just sat there smiling
sipping a dark beer
enjoying it
watching me go sweaty and crazy
knowing that we'd both end up at the same place.
And that's what I learned
after my youth passed me by.
I wanted to be great, but never proved it
with anything more than words,
and by thirty-five the only thing I was running on
was caffeine.
Tom wanted to be the best average person
he could be
and always had been
since the day I'd met him.
And as much as I hate people
who have figured out how to be happy,
Tom is one
who I think deserves it.

Heroes

They talk a lot about heroes now
because the world has none.
The kids can't go to bed
without kissing the TV goodnight
and after the first mistake
and two marriage-savers are tucked in
Mom stays up five extra minutes
to thank Jesus. She lifts the blanket
and Dad's fart from earlier
is finally free. He's asleep and she thinks
about how easy it would be to put a
screwdriver through his neck.

She takes an Ambien from the drawer
and hopes for a good night's sleep.
Warm thoughts of murder and
petting zoos take over.
But she wakes up early anyway and
drives to the gym for yoga at sunrise.
Why did she marry Riley
instead of going to that retreat in Taos?

She asks herself this in a parking lot
until her friends catch up
for brunch. For eggs and vodka. To
show pictures of their kids and complain
about the refugee problem.
Like we don't all die in the same twilight.
These parades of marching bands
and zeppoles
where do they go
once Sixth Avenue ends?

Home?
To Staten Island?
When did they become mothers
who strap their babies in and drive
silver minivans to the petting zoo?
Who save quarters all week for
the cereal machine
so the zebras can eat breakfast?

The days roll by like slow tumbleweeds now.
They remember what it was like
to live in the city.
Subways always late.
Trenches surrounding the boroughs
like an aquarium of old condoms
sturgeon confuse for jellyfish.

But they can afford the vacation upstate.
And every summer they rent a house.
And they can see the town
crying harder each year.
They sell booze now where
the sneaker store was.
Raccoons roam the park.
The kids can't run through the forest this summer
because the bees never found the flowers.
And it'll always be like this.
The happy days were here once, but not now.
They were the last generation
to write history books full of heroes.
But they didn't save us.
And the kids get detention
if they talk about them
anymore.

V.

HAWAIIAN SHIRTS IN THE ELECTRIC CHAIR

(Written in Hazlet, NJ)

I Wish This Didn't Happen

Remember when you got the guts
to tell me
I'd never be happy?
While you were crying
and naked
waiting for me to understand
what you already knew?
It was the moment
I realized
I'd always be alone.
I said you were crazy
but a better man
would have called it
bravery.
I can remember your diary
on the floor
lying like a bone,
the inside of you
showing itself to me.
You weren't an artist but
I'll bet a younger you
wanted to be.
And I remember I
only had a hoodie for
the walk home.
The smoke trailed out of
my mouth
from your front door to
my back porch.

The time after that
when you took me back

you asked me,
"Why can't this
just be easy?"

I wanted you to understand
it was never meant to be
that way.
We were just actors
playing characters
on a cold stage.
No notes
or method
or clear understanding
of why the curtain
always falls
exactly
the same way.

We were born under the same moon.
Shared the same bad sign.
And it worked for a while
because you saw life
for what it could be
and I saw life
for what it was.
But there's no peace
for people like me.
All those hours you spent
smiling in your sleep
I knew *they* were closing in.
So I never slept.
And I wondered about
my home in the sky
or my hole

in the ground.

I hope you know
what I know now.
That *they* were closing in for you.
But it wasn't
to take you.
They built a wall around you
that showed itself sometimes.
When light fought its way
through leaves and
windows
and under doors
like carpets
to warm your feet.
It was never easy
because I never
had faith in anything.
I was just like the rest of them.
And I loved you
because
you weren't
like any of them.

I forgot about all that.
And light was always around,
I just never noticed
until it stopped
shining on us.

Wait For It

There's not a high enough hill on earth to stand on and scream for God. I can see you. Above the trees. A long blue sky with big fleece clouds. Pointing your finger straight up. Demanding first salvation, then a few dollars, and finally, just acknowledgment. But He never shows. How can that surprise you? You were never able to get us on the ground to stop laughing at you. You think God is going to turn the television down?

Autumn, A Finish Line

Twenty years ago we dragged the flame
along the knife.
You, me, opening our forearms and kissing the river.
To let love in –
to be twenty and know all there is to know.
Your spit, a communion, a movie on the TV,
bleeding together all night, and now we bleed alone.
On stage they called you Autumn, you were their
favorite, you were mine too, but there was a theft, an
empty chamber, and now when I see your mother's
house I wonder what precious thing
backed all that currency,
and were you ever worth a broken back
or even real at all?
It's autumn now, but the leaves are still green.
It's a desert always, even when the trees are full
and Brooklyn sinks a little lower with each new rain.
I think about words that leave their root and become
a philosophy - the desert, Wall Street, love, America,
and my favorite - Las Vegas. Remember the chapel
where the dead came back to life and
Buddy Holly sang the requiem to a future
many have tried
but we were going to beat them all?
A black veil. A highway back to New Jersey.
A couch with a dog. A plant in the window.
A good life.
Now I'm seeing forty and I know nothing
except that everything ends,
and when you look back a decade or so later
you can't even be sure it was really you
who went through it.

Turnpike Blues

He looked at me
as uninterested
and defeated as a twenty-five year old
on his way to a shitty job
in a shitty town
could, and asked,
"Have you ever thought about a necktie?
I mean ... why?"
It was a question someone
who hasn't spent hours
driving alone
to somewhere they didn't want to go
would never understand.
    I looked at the landscape of the
New Jersey Turnpike, right at the
starting line of what was sure to be
another dead
and eternal winter, and
the air stunk like a chemically enhanced
napalm fart.
    Then I looked down at my necktie,
hoping somehow it wouldn't be there.
    It was.
I was a manufactured monkey like everyone else.

I lit a cigarette to dilute
the fart smell.
Ernest and I exchanged a silent nod.
    We worked an
    hour later than was scheduled.

Jersey Shore

There you were
on that Jersey sand
in a white bikini
like Marilyn Monroe
pinned up on a teenager's wall
or in a jail cell
over a fresh coat of paint.
A girl from a different era
when everything was good
and no sea turtles
swallowed six-pack rings
and I could take my baby
down The Parkway
to the casino lights
on a Saturday night.

You'd heard about me
but we were Kings and Queens
so I asked you out anyway.
And you looked back at your friends'
shaking heads
and saw that they cared about your sanity
not your happiness
so you said yes.
I knew forever
could start like that
so I made a mixtape for the drive
and picked you up at seven.
You were a dream I'd been saving
since my first life
and your mother
saw it on my face when

she answered the doorbell,
so she sent you out
into a stranger's arms
and didn't worry like she used to.

I remember your high score at the arcade
and the four free pinballs
that dropped in
when you broke the last record.
There wasn't much you were bad at,
at least I can't remember anything now,
and how about that sunrise
over the Asbury waves
when we bummed a cigarette
and squinted our eyes into darkness
while the sun took the night
and gave us back our youth?

You told your friends about
every bad night in our book.
I'll bet they never heard of that perfect one.

From Here To LA

We drove from here to LA
in total silence
because Ace Enders
said we should.
Of course
he talked for hours,
actually he just screamed
(and he did it for hours)
into a cell phone
as he paced around the trailer
in the parking lot of every gas station
  from here to LA.

He wrote his best songs at his worst.
After the phone calls
with his soulmate.
(She liked the attention
even if she never understood her artist)
But if she didn't tear him apart
he never would've written those songs,
and I wouldn't have fallen asleep each night
listening to him
pick the guitar strings
singing about the love he would see
when we finally sold enough merch
to fly her
  from there to LA.

His hair grew long.
(He was the converse-wearing all-star)
He grew out his beard.
(Mad whiskers on a mad dog)

Somewhere between Wind Gap and Winnemucca
we became a tribe,
and Ace
wore the feathered headdress.
It was never spoken of,
never decided,
but he was the man for that place
and time.
And the other bands knew it too.
We weren't the headliners,
we didn't draw the biggest crowds,
but the other bands hushed
when Ace walked into the room –
we all knew we were treading
with a real songwriter.
But HE DIDN'T KNOW IT,
would never accept it,
and I watched him go mad
trying to write
the book of love
and recite it each night
to the girl on the cell phone
in every parking lot of
every gas station
    from here to LA.

Half the band watched
The Karate Kid on repeat.
The rest of us read road novels
and listened to Wilco.
    But not Ace!
He just stared out the window
and occasionally jumped up and screamed
until his face got hot and red,

and then he'd quiet down
    and start staring again.

In Portland
Ace and I walked across the city
to find a Post Office.
The mental institutions had just run out of funds
and all the crazies were released onto the streets.
One grabbed Ace's shirt,
and like a zoo animal does when you catch it
staring at you,
he looked right into Ace's soul
and said, "I know what you did."
I knew
that he knew,
whatever it was,
no matter how nuts the bum was,
that he really knew what Ace had done,
even if I didn't know
Ace had ever done anything.
Ace asked me if I thought it was possible.
I didn't ask what he had done
but I told him
that the bum probably knew.
And even though Ace said he didn't like attention
he thought it was a good story,
and he asked everyone that question
    from there to LA.

They called him a mad genius.
They called him a crazy artist.
They called him a possessed songwriter.
    I'm not really sure of any of those things
because it took a woman to make him crazy

and a country to drive him insane,
but on Monday morning most people
still have to get up and
go to work.
    I do know that all it takes to make a
beautiful brain crumble
is a woman
pushing the 'ignore' button
on the other end of the cell phone.
And it can happen in less time
than it takes
    to drive from here to LA.

Lorraine

I didn't know she was drunk
until
she threw up across her desk.
They say, "Don't write about love
because it's lame
because it's all been said before
because by now
everyone knows it doesn't exist."

But this was it.
The real thing.
All the burning
and desires.
The smell of Rhone.
The smell of rain.
She wretched back and forth
as the fish tank lights of fluorescent classrooms
found their subject.
The rest of the class sat in front of their computers
like rookies in a police academy.
Obedient.
Loyal.
Sipping cups of coffee for a clarity
that wouldn't come,
becoming machines in hopes of not being
replaced by them.
Like the scabs who cross picket lines.
Like the prisoner of war who builds bullets.
Getting a paycheck today to extinct tomorrow.

But not her.
She is a rebel

in a time
where cool has died,
and the new revolution
won't be televised
but you'll pay monthly to subscribe.

And in an age where everyone gets a microphone
but no one's read a book,
sometimes
all it takes is public vomiting
to prove
that you are still free.

You Just Can't Win or A Poem For Lindsay Lohan's Personal Assistant

When you move to Manhattan
you meet a lot of people
(mainly women)
who come from "means."
They hang out in the marble lobbies
of boutique hotels
and drink fancy cocktails
and talk a lot of shit.

I met a girl on the job
who started a "non-profit"
where basically
you asked your parents
not to give you any Christmas gifts.
Instead,
you had them donate the gift money
to the "non-profit" on Christmas morning
that one year,
and from there it went to whatever
tragedy du jour was in fashion
with her famous friends.

Our first date (our only date)
went fine.
She liked country music
so we found a karaoke bar
and got drunk and sang
Taylor Swift songs.
She said we sounded like a real band
and when I asked her
if she wanted to go to the waterfront

and look at the skyline
she said,
"My bedroom has a better view."

Later, I sat with a cigarette
on her roof top patio
overlooking all of
downtown Manhattan
and
I thought about how nice
life was to those who could
forfeit their Christmas money
and still pay rent on an apartment
with a roof top patio
that overlooked
all of
downtown Manhattan.

Eventually, I had to leave
and I ate for the first time
that day
the one piece of dollar pizza
I could scum up enough
change to buy.
And all around me were
one-legged bums
and
Mexican families with seven kids
and the short black man
with no teeth
who sang The Lollipop Guild song
for some loot.

And I knew I'd never be her hero.

And it wasn't even winter -
every half-frozen puddle
I stomped through broke apart,
and when
the ripples
came back together
it was still my stupid face
I was staring at.

She may have been the savior
of the damned
but the next morning I got
a text message that said,
"You're really nice,
but I can't date a bellman.
It just wouldn't look right."

It was another night
I abandoned my dog
for a woman
that I'd never get back.

A Girl From Greenwich Village

It's about time I came over.
Before the plane disappeared
and the bombs dropped
and the dog parks emptied
with fresh coats
falling over soiled snow.
Everyone following single file
over the cliff,
but we don't have to.
You've got the book of love now.
I left it on your coffee table
blank of opinion.
There's a pen on the floor,
use it,
I won't walk away.
Use it,
while the thought of me
still exorcises
the loneliness in you.
Please fill those pages now.
I know you will when the
yellow birds fly away,
but I want you to remember me
like this -
carrying you over
the garbage piles
on Thompson Street,
frozen over like igloos
for the rats.

It's about time I came over.
For coffee at midnight.

For sunrise bedtime.
Remember me spilling wine
on your couch
and ducking pigeons
on your stoop.
You've got the pen,
use it.
You saved me from that place
I go all the time
but barely mention.
I thought it would be a new guitar
or a better job
or a poem highlighted
in a used book.
But it never is.
Just a look from the girl
who was
never broken by the world.
A runny nose
and an underserved smile
was all it took to escape
the firing squad of my mind.

Buffalo Bones

An unsmoked cigarette
burns for thirteen minutes
without a drag.
And since you're all grown up now
there must be a wedding day.
The town will throw you a parade,
rope off the streets where tanks
have rolled
and teenagers did *The Hokey Pokey*
after Sunday Mass.
They'll re-introduce you to the
man who baptized you.
He says The Lord's Prayer often
but it doesn't
sound familiar.

The blimp banner clocks the national debt
but nothing about all the I.O.U.'s
for last month's rent.
Or how fast cigarettes burn
as you sit around counting hours.
An arc of time is never real until
your lover pulls the joker.
You're all in, full ante,
and one hand later
the game is over.

You know it then.
They lied to you but that's okay.
It just hurts real bad
when the rules change
and your professors

still want the homework.
Maybe Santa will pay the late fees
if you say grace every day of Lent.

Pull out the old box of maps
from under your bed.
Get your revolver loaded and
pick a direction,
a spot on the map
you've never been before.
Hitchhike to the Dakotas
where the weather's colder.
Where strangers with no faces
stand over your shoulders
counting pages in your notebook.
The wolves run free.
No swings in the park.
Maybe the buffalo jumped the cliff for fun,
left their bleached white skulls in the pits
looking up.
They're hidden until the thaw.
That's when you'll find them grinning
with the spring bloom.
Don't worry,
eventually
we all shiver
in the sun.

VI.

PSYOP HOPSCOTCH

(Written in California)

EWR - LAX

Plane lands
Doors unopened
All the bovine stand

Looking At The Silver Lake

I kiss the dream goodbye in Silver Lake
while drinking Georgian wine with Austin.
The sun has already left Echo Park
and now it hangs over us like the eye
of a hollow sphinx,
briefly,
and it drizzles over the ripples in the lake
like little lines of milk for the ducks.
Their heads dip under the surface of
the Silver Lake in formation,
safe behind the black-chain fence.

A silent movie star lived in the house behind us,
my feet are up on his old porch
and we're staring at the houses in the rising hills
across the water,
lights filling their windows like the teeth
of a big smiling clown,
or the dreams I hear about that sometimes
make my girlfriend laugh in her sleep.

"It looks like Italy over there," I say to Austin.
"Everyone says that," he sighs. "I've never been."
I haven't either, but I know
this stretch of desert
can't be paralleled or compared
after these last six months of rain.
The Jade Trees are spitting up
white spiderwebs of flowers.
The hummingbirds so blue
a storybook must've freed them.
I watch a lizard hug a green leaf and somehow

in my empty pack two fresh cigarettes appear.

Austin hands me the wine and looks for a lighter.
We are young in California.
We are poor with Georgian wine and
the Silver Lake ducks.
There is a party at midnight
we have no chance of making.

If only tomorrow wouldn't come.
If only the sun knew what it did.
The light will be clean but this night
will already be a memory,
and the plans for next time
will ruminate with the eras
that found these hills long before us.
Locked in a bird call or a rock etching.
A language I know but never speak.
A foreigner praying to be left behind.

Hummingbird Hill

You wake up most mornings to ambulances
to your neighbor on the phone with her mother
to the package guy buzzing at the door
to your dog needing to take a piss
to the landlord assessing the square footage
of your apartment
to the building next-door getting ripped down
to the cement truck reversing in to fill it back up

But sometimes you wake up
to hummingbirds in Los Angeles,
multiplying after each rain and bringing
the whole family line to your bush.
And you come alive off a stranger's couch,
knock over a bottle of wine,
rub last night out of your eyes
and look through a kitchen window
with an oil painting of an orange grove
right next to it.
And there they are.
Twenty green and blue hummingbirds.
The sound of their small engines lulls you to a place
where your hangover hibernates for a while.
And they play and dodge and hit the flowers
like a dogfight where everyone's on the same team.
And you lie back on the couch and all you want to do
is smell your girlfriend's neck.
And even though it's been ten years
you want to make love with her right there
on the living room floor.

There is so little you want
but you don't know how to ask for it.
Can you package your treasure
and take it back to New York?
It took almost forty years to get here
and you stopped.
There is so little you want
and still they won't let you have it.
You've got a girl in New York and you came here.
You can package your treasure, sure,
but this spring can't last forever.
Did you call her last night and ask how her day was?
You get one shot at a second chance
and a whole lifetime to ruin it.

Hollywood Rain

You started off looking for Rome like I did.
In poems, in love letters,
written for a city planes fly to every day
but you knew
or decided
you hadn't earned it yet.
So you went to West Hollywood,
a walk each night down Sunset,
not exactly The Malecón
or The Rue des Rosiers
but the girls are skinny
and sometimes you follow the one
with the German Shepherd
up Rodeo
to a house her father couldn't afford
until they painted the walls
with Sharon and her baby.
The neighbor's thought a murder
would sink the value but they forgot
the California sun can
baptize anything.
And when the tourists come
she puts her yoga mat in front of the bay window,
falling into downward dog
like she doesn't know what she's doing.
And the men snap pictures of her
stretched out on this cursed land,
almost as rare
as a Hollywood rain
but nowhere near as beautiful.

The Forced Encore (For Conor Oberst)

You were a kid once
and named songs like epitaphs
because the gun
was always against your head
and the white keys
weren't enough back then.
But the Gods are unkind
and the streets crack from wheels
dragging under old steel.

The crowds count down now
but the fat lady never sings.
There was a poem
you put into every song
about an early death
because
like a warmer winter or a Gideons Bible
life rarely seems like a gift.
And when the lights come on
the crowd still has some beer
in their cups,
they paid the cover;
your sweat wasn't enough.

Get back out there.
Pull the ghosts from the 8-track.
You can sleep tomorrow as the van
pulls headfirst into a sunrise
and somewhere long ago
you might remember a kid
whose only dream was this life.

In Front Of The Closed Formosa Cafe

they'll tell you "it's your life"
and either all of it is
or none of it is,
that's up to you.
they won't tell you this is all
one big nothing, though,
and eventually you'll stop
starting something new
because you're ashamed of them
finding out you quit again.
it's the ones who say they love you
that'll scare you the most,
they know something about you,
they'll use it to hurt you.
and when the cards fall
the faults don't split straight,
as anyone under the mushroom cloud
will admit.

so make your choice soon.

or don't.

fallen trees and most suicides
have marched quietly
into the silent night.

Outer Sunset

There's a ghost ship beyond
the breakers of Ocean Beach,
and this low tide dragged far out
makes it look even larger and more haunted.
Everything in San Francisco sounds
like a movie or a song you've heard only once
and exists on the periphery
nameless and glowing
in a way only the past can refine.

The sidewalk down Outer Sunset
is filled with new parents and their new children.
My girlfriend has to drop my hand to let them pass.
And of course I see her eyes,
lighting up her face like an exhibit in a showroom,
watching life and family breeze between the two of us
until our hands join again.

I know what I've taken from her.
I'm selfish,
my hourglass never far from my thoughts.
But she's a reef,
a million mouths could've fed from her.

On the black sand of this shore,
the end of America,
I want to stick my knee in the surf and ask her.
It's the only thing I haven't asked of her.
How can I make up for the years she's spent
in Harlem? In Williamsburg?
Waiting while I get into someone's car and drive west,
always chasing something that takes and never gives,

vanishing for a month
while the only thing that matters
sits patiently at home.
I've known since birth a good life
wasn't in my cards,
but couldn't I give one to someone else?

And there she is, the center of all life,
kicking the surf with cold water goose bumps.
Children laughing in the sand around her.
Dogs with no leashes charging the small waves.
The last wildflower between me and
the ghost ship no one ever sees.

I had to reach the other side to
put a period on my life.
The Pacific baptizing all my second chances.
California still the promised land.
The last poem I'll ever write,
never to begin again.

"I was born a dirt poor man
all my life I had hard-working hands
so I sang my songs as I carried my load
because I had a dream about Rainbow Road."

- K.K.

BONE

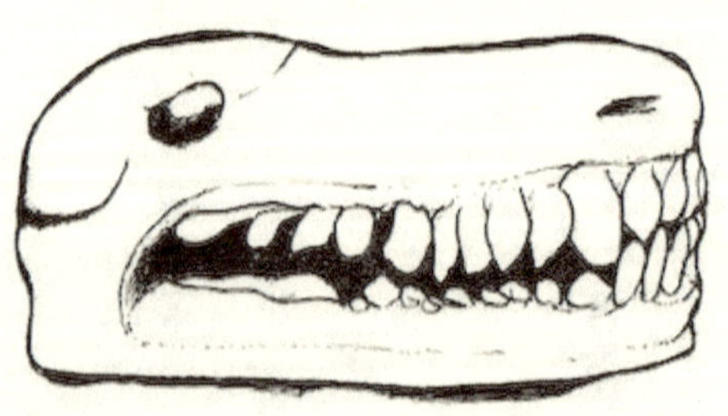

MACHINE

www.ingramcontent.com/pod-product-compliance
Lightning Source LLC
LaVergne TN
LVHW090528110826
845146LV00003B/1016

* 9 7 9 8 2 3 4 0 6 6 5 5 8 *